T0065460

101 WAYS TO MAKE A LIVING FLYING SEAPLANES

HOW, WHERE, HOW MUCH

PAT MAGIE

authorHOUSE

AuthorHouse™
1663 Liberty Drive
Bloomington, IN 47403
www.authorhouse.com
Phone: 833-262-8899

Published by AuthorHouse 03/08/2021

ISBN: 978-1-6655-1751-5 (sc)
ISBN: 978-1-6655-1750-8 (e)

Library of Congress Control Number: 2021903389

Print information available on the last page.

This book is printed on acid-free paper.

CONTENTS

CHAPTER 1

GETTING STARTED

I consider myself very lucky in life by making my living doing what I liked to do best — which was flying and doing the kind of flying I liked best. I found out that this entitled me to work seven days a week — and flying ten to twelve hours a day. Thirteen and one half hours was my maximum and I hit that several times. This would not win friends or influence members of the FAA, but I did it for 63 years and 40,800 hours without any problems. One of the neat benefits was that most of the flights were short — sometimes only minutes. No long days sitting there watching the auto pilot get all the fun — or some unknown non-pilot on the ground telling me what to do. I always hated IFR — even though I was a CFII. I remember coming out of NW Chicago one night, with a customer's Cessna 310 that I had taken there for some avionics maintenance in some pretty lousy weather. I filed direct IFR to Beloit, Wisconsin, then north to Janesville, Wisconsin, and Madison. I was plugging along at 6,000 feet when Center came up with a change in the sector frequency and the words "direct Janesville when able". I turned the VOR to Janesville and got a strong signal and turned to it. Then I checked in with Center "6,000". A few minutes later Center told me that I was considerably off course. I told the gal that my needle was centered, but I would certainly watch it. Five minutes later she came back on frequency and said she was going to file a violation on me for being so far off course. I replied that I had two VOR needles absolutely centered — then the light

1

bulb came on over my head. I told her that the previous sector had told me to proceed direct to Janesville when able — which I did before checking in with the next sector. I got a "standby". A few minutes later she called back saying I was good to go. I certainly have to say that I enjoyed a radio-less environment — then any mistakes are mine. When we first went to Hawaii I had 30,000 hours of flight time with no memorable incidents of a mid-air, but early on in one 30 minute tour I had three cases of traffic that was given to me under control each time within 1 ½ mile, once at USMC Class Delta airspace and twice in HNL Class Bravo, two helicopters and one JAL DC-10. I did learn not to trust anyone.

I really liked seaplane flying and did a lot of flight training for both single engine seaplane and multi-engine sea. I would have to say that about 95% of my trainees thought it was the most fun of flying, but hard to get into for a career. Just to qualify for being hired by a operating seaplane company, requires quite a bit of experience to meet the insurance minimums. I had bought a Piper J-4 Cub Coupe, a set of Edo 1320 floats and skis for less than $3,000 and learned how to fly on floats. I soloed on floats and got my private license on floats. A year later I sold the Cub for a slight profit and purchased a Stinson 108-3 with floats, skis and wheels for $5,500.00. Now I learned about carrying canoes, boats and other external loads as well as more passengers. At 485 flight hours I took my commercial pilot check ride in my Stinson N602G. I made an appointment with Ned Powers at Grand Rapids — a hours flight away. I got there about 9:00 a.m. and we did a quick inspection of the aircraft and logbooks followed by an hours oral session. Then we flew for a hour and a half doing take—offs and landings, aerial maneuvers, step turns, high speed taxi, sailing and docking which all went pretty slick. When Ned did the paperwork, he was surprised to see that I did not have a land plane rating. He said that he had seen me hopping rides at the ice fishing contests on skis during the winter which required a land plane rating. He made me an offer that for $85.00 we could rent a Cessna 172 on the field and do three take—off and landings and he could sign off my commercial single engine land also. We did it and it was interesting — this was the first time I had ever flown an airplane on wheels and with brakes!

Three years later I sold the Stinson for a $500.00 profit and bought a low time 1955 Cessna 180 (N4636B) for $12,500.00 on Edo 2870 floats. Then I made a large step forward and purchased the property I had been leasing that had a fair sized dock, an older 60 foot by 60 foot hanger. I also got 37 acres of property with 3,300 feet of shoreline with a well treed point sticking out into Shagawa Lake.

This had been owned by a iron mining company out of Duluth, Minnesota. They had an operating underground iron mine there for almost 30 years when the product ran out. The mine shaft was located about a third of a mile from the lake shore lot that I purchased for $15,000.00 and they carried the paper for ten years. Another seaplane operator leased this property for his operation after WWII ended, but he was forced out of business in June of 1953 when the NE part of Minnesota was turned into a no fly wilderness area reserved for canoe parties. Bill Leithold was his name and one of four seaplane operators on Shagawa Lake. At that time he had been using two J-3 Cubs, an Aeronca Champ, a Fairchild 51 and a Noorduyn Norseman on floats in the summer and skis in the winter. He had built a 60ft. x 60ft hanger, metal covered, but with a dirt floor and 16 foot high walls of 2"x4" material. I immediately got busy and traded out a local contracting company some fly in fishing to dig out another 20 feet of space at the back end of the hanger. We then built an addition to the hanger using 2"x6" material this time which now gave me a 60ft wide by 80ft deep hanger. Then I got hold of a concrete operator who I had flown several times and offered a Canadian Moose hunting trip for two people in trade for pouring a six inch concrete floor. This got done very quickly while I made a partial trade out with a local lumber yard for a fly-in fishing trip for a Sunday for four persons, with a picnic dinner for some lumber and insulation.

Meanwhile we added another 16 foot 2"x4" stud to every other one and doubled every other rafter. I could not find a trade for the furnace, but I bought one so we now had a winterized hanger which made life much simpler when it was—40 degrees below zero. A couple years later I added a two story office on the south side which gave us a counter, waiting room, parts room and my office downstairs, and up stairs was a classroom and men's and women's restrooms — each with a shower so that guests could clean up before heading for home as well as space for a small coffee shop and deck overlooking the dock. We put up walls of maps so that people could look at them and plan their next years trip. I did a lot of trade-outs as I did not have a bundle of cash to get things done. We always tried to fly a trade-out in when we could pick up a paying party on the return or vice versa. This allowed me to do a lot of things which might have been too expensive otherwise. Later on a few years when I was working in Alaska we worked quite a few sport and boat shows around the U.S. during the winter months. I would usually contact one of the larger auto sales outlets who had a staff of salesmen — sometimes at a couple of sites. I would make the offer to provide a week of Alaska fishing for a group of four persons for a $10,000.00 to $12,000.00 credit on a new Suburban or pickup. They would have a 30 day sales contest that would usually bring in a good batch of units sold. Sometimes we would make an even trade for a clean used vehicle. One time we traded a one week tour of Alaska for two persons for a houseboat rental for the winter in Stockton, California — plus we got several fully paid for trips later as referrals. Trade outs are not liked by the IRS, but I sure liked them.

In the early 70's I found an add in Trade-A-Plane offering an Aero Commander 500 aircraft for sale for $26,000.00 with financing available. I called the seller to get the specifics which he readily gave me and faxed me a couple of photos. This was the model with a pair of 250 h.p. Lycoming engines like the Piper Aztec — 2,000 hours between overhaul, pretty dependable and seven seats which makes a pilot and six passengers. I thought about this for a couple of hours until I called the bank who held the mortgage to see about the financing. Surprisingly I got hold of a fellow I knew, Bruce Pendy. He used to work in a bank in St. Paul, Minnesota and I had financed several aircraft with him before he moved out to the East Coast. Thus it only took five minutes to set up the financing for five years with me air mailing a $6,000.00 check for the down payment. I picked up Commander N180M a few days later to bring it back to Minnesota. In the next two years we did over 40 multi-engine land ratings — including five for myself and staff — plus a few hundred hours of charter. The only major expense was the exchange of one engine for $15,000.00. Returning from a charter flight to northern Indiana one day I flew over a grass landing strip just NE of Grand Rapids, Michigan that had a DeHavilland Beaver along with a DeHavilland DHC-3 Otter tied down. Both were still painted in OD military colors. I immediately swung around, landed and taxied into an office and hanger. I was told that this field belonged to the Grand Rapids Bible and Music School that taught missionary pilots how to fly. They did say that the headmaster was ex-Air Force and had arranged a transfer of two surplus Beavers and Two Otters for the cost of $20.00 each for the bill of sale and registration. Then they took me out to the hanger where the others were stored disassembled. The assembled Otter was used to fly their band around to perform at concerts. They also had a tricycle gear Champion as a primary trainer. The headmaster was gone for two days, but I got his name and phone number. I did get hold of him and suggested a trade, I would give him a brand new Cessna 150 on wheels, a two year old low time Cessna 172 on wheels, a five year old 1,200 hour Cessna 185 with wheels, a set of Fluidyne wheel skis plus a set of PK amphibious floats and to top it off the Aero Commander 500 for the assembled Beaver and Otter plus the unassembled and uncertified Beaver and Otter in the hanger. I thought that this would be a good deal for training missionary pilots for flying with wheel, ski, seaplane and multi engine experience. He agreed with me, but said he had to get the approval from the Board of Directors then get back to me. A week later he called and said there was no approval, so I offered to trade the Aero Commander for the disassembled Otter. This offer was accepted a few days later, so I sent a truck and our 40 foot trailer down there to pick the Otter up and towed it to Seattle to have it rebuilt and certified. A month later we picked it up, flew it back, got it painted, on floats and working.

The Otter was quite an aircraft — 11 seats, over a seven hour range and really made short take-off and landings with almost 2,900 pounds of useful load. Over 450 units were built between 1951 and 1967. A few months later I won a bid on another Otter at a military surplus auction in Norfolk, Virginia for $32,000.00. This was assembled and complete except for a missing RH rear door. The van and trailer went on the road again to haul it to Mena, Arkansas. Mena was a small town, but the airport was amazing with 17 aircraft repair shops, two engine overhaul ops, a radio shop, a upholstery shop and two paint shops. These people bought a lot of damaged aircraft from the insurance companies, then rebuilt them to resell. It was quite a busy airport for a town of 5,000 people. That fall when the season started to wind-down I put the Otter N432GR up for sale because N90626 would be flying soon. I advertised it with a price of $170,000.00 and got a call from a doctor in Anchorage, Alaska who wanted to trade-in a Beechcraft Queen Air 80. We negotiated for a few days to finally agree on the Queen Air and $55,000.00 with a meeting in Seattle to switch the aircraft — halfway for each of us. I got the Queen Air back to Ely as winter started. I put it up for sale immediately, but it did not have hot props or deicing boots so there was no serious interest, but we did several multiengine ratings in it. In the spring I delivered it to Florida to sell it to a broker which got me almost $110,000.00. That $6,000.00 down pay on the Commander started it all. We flew the Commander almost 800 revenue hours in two years, close to 500 hours in the Otter N432GR, 150 hours in the Otter N9062G, 150 hours in the Otter N90627 plus almost 1,000 revenue hours in the Queen Air.

For a while in Honolulu we belonged to a trade club. They would sell our flights for points that we could use at different hotels and restaurants along with printing and other services. One of the major problems of starting a seaplane business is finding waterfront property that is suitable as well as affordable. A residential area will raise a lot of objections due to the noise level. If you can find a operating airport that is located with one side on water — a lake, river, reservoir or ocean you may have a chance to lease some waterfront in an area that is already zoned for aircraft use. Again if you offer to build your own floating office and dock, the door may open to get a reasonable lease. Definitely register the office as a homemade boat. This will give you a legal right to park where other boats are allowed as well as probably eliminate property tax expense. We were in Hawaii for 23 years with our floating office and wedding chapel registered as vessels and we paid $20.00 per year for each for the boat tags, but no property taxes. We had put in a bedroom and kitchen/pantry so that we could be 24 hour security after we came to work several mornings to find that someone had been crawling around in the aircraft during the night. We also had two restrooms along with a shower on the outside dock with a holding tank that was pumped out once a week. The office was 20 feet wide and 40 feet long with a 10 foot by 10 foot bedroom, a 10 foot by 10 foot kitchen pantry, a 8 foot by 15 foot private office which left us a 20 foot by 22 foot counter area and waiting room that easily seated 16 people. The dock was constructed of 4"X12" beams and covered with 2"X12" planks and was 225 feet long and 30 feet wide. This width would allow an aircraft as large as a DeHavilland DHC 6 Twin Otter to park with plenty of wing clearance with the floating office. The dock itself was hinged to the shore with two 20 foot wide by 30 feet long ramps that were hinged to two bulkheads on the shore side. That allowed the dock and buildings to go up and down with the tide and even hurricanes and Tsunamis. We even built a 20 foot by 24 foot floating wedding chapel attached behind the dock and leased out to a Japanese Wedding company. This was a pretty good source of income with up to 700 weddings a year. We gave the bride and groom a 20 minute seaplane tour down to over fly Diamondhead and back over Pearl Harbor. We built the dock with two 20 foot by 20 foot pneumatic hinged ramps that we could taxi the airplanes up on and hook up an air compressor to get them out of the water when not in use. This is not too important in fresh water, but it saves a lot of barnacle scraping and corrosion when in salt water. We leased a 50 foot wide by 300 feet long piece of land from the Airports Division of the State of Hawaii, but it took us eight years to complete the lease from my first inquiry. It was a strange lease being with a 30 day revocable clause. It did not take too long for wife Debbie with a green thumb to get potted palm trees along with flowers and plants along the dock. We also built three eight foot tables and benches so that people could sit there to watch the airplanes take off and land. These would also be used during our evening meal deals.

The parties were very popular with quite a few companies that wanted to do something special for their employees — especially during holiday periods. We often would have my oldest daughter send some fresh halibut and salmon on the airlines from Alaska so we could serve deep fried beer battered halibut, and charcoaled salmon with potato salad. The hosting company would normally provide some wine or beer. Everyone got a 20 minute sight seeing ride — which for almost everyone would be their first time flying off the water. We always heard that they were surprised that the landings were so soft.

When you get ready with all of the other steps taken care of you will definitely want to contact Merco Marine of Wellsburg, West Virginia — www.mercoboatdocks.com to get a copy of their catalog. They offer just about everything you will need for the project including very sturdy hardware, a great selection of vinyl covered foam blocks for floatation as well as strong lift tanks. These meet all Corps of Engineers regulations as well as having a 15 year warranty. You will probably want to look for the best deal on lumber close to home. While we were in Alaska we purchased a band sawmill that we could dismantle to put in either the Beaver or Twin Beech 18. Then we would fly 50 or 60 miles down the coast to find a batch of cedar logs that get loose from one of the logging companies and blew up on the beach. Then we would camp there for a few days to produce lumber and stack it up. Whenever we had an empty flight coming back to town we would stop to pick up a load. We got quite a bit of very reasonably priced lumber for docks and buildings and sold the sawmill later.

There are several facets for making an income with a seaplane. The two most common are sightseeing rides or seaplane flight training. I bought my own airplane on floats and hired a fellow to teach me how to fly. I soloed on floats in eight hours, got my Private License on floats a year and one half later with almost two hundred hours of flight time. I got serious about the Private License after someone leaked it to the Canadian Customs officer that I only had a student pilot's certificate which states right on it that no international flights are permitted. I only lived ten minutes flying time from the Canadian border, so I was making quite a few day trips into Canada for fishing. Once I got shut down, I took the written exam followed by the check ride on floats. Then I could start fishing again. I would fly into Ontario for an hour or so, land in a remote lake that had a river flowing into it, drop a small anchor and fish while standing on a float. I think the catch limit in those days was eight Walleyed Pike that I would take home for dinner, dispensing one to the Canadian Customs Officer plus one to the U.S. Customs agent in Ely when he checked me in at my arrival at the dock. I have to admit to cheating after that. I was 200 miles to the nearest FAA office — GADO in those days. So I occasionally would take a couple of people for a short sightseeing flight and even take two passengers and a canoe to flyout in the morning and get picked up that evening after fishing. I had my Stinson 108-3 then which did a pretty good job while teaching me a lot. During the winter months on skis I would hop 15 minute rides at the ice fishing contests each Sunday with sometimes 5,000 people and their vehicles on the ice. A new car was often awarded as first prize for the largest fish caught. I had almost 500 hours flight time and I took my commercial pilot check ride which convinced me to purchase a low time 1955 Cessna 180 on floats for $12,500.00 — and get a FAA Part 135 Certificate to become legal. Amazingly that check ride was the first time that I have ever flown an airplane on Wheels and brakes, so that I would have both a commercial land and sea rating!

ADDING A CESSNA 206 ON LINE

CHAPTER 2

SIGHTSEEING BUSINESS

One of the easiest ways to start a seaplane business is sightseeing. A sightseeing operation gives you a lot of choice in the aircraft used in your business. Probably it is hard to beat a Cessna 172 to start with.

It should be at least a 1968 or later when the Lycoming engines were first used. Then for a large difference in load carrying it should be a 180 h.p. engine conversion and a fixed pitch propeller. This fixed pitch is lighter than the constant speed at the forward balance point and usually has longer blades.

It will be a little slower, but that usually is not much of a problem on sightseeing tours. It should definitely have the rear child's seat and a larger float then the Edo 2000 which was originally approved.

This allows you to fly a 30 minute tour for a family of four or five including two or three children up to 100 pounds or so —father 165 lbs, mother 135 .bs, child one 90 lbs, child two 65 lbs, child three 54 lbs, one hour fuel 10 gallons = 565 lbs including 30 minute reserve. You could offer a reduced rate for the children if you wish (maybe ½ price). I always operated with the 30 minute reserve in the RH tank and the fuel for each flight in the LH side or dock side — never fill tanks. If you cannot find one with the child's seat installed, it is not too bad of a job to buy one and install it, but they are a great money maker.

You should definitely have larger floats than the original Edo 2000's with the passenger weight moved aft. I prefer a flat top over Edo's round top — much easier for both you and your passengers to move around on. There is the Aerocet 2200 (composite), Aqua 2400 and PK 2300. I have owned 488 aircraft in my life and about only half a dozen amphibs and had a commitment when I ordered them. I do not like the weight difference or reduction in performance — and especially the difference in insurance premiums! To me a seaplane is a seaplane and if I wanted a land plane I would buy one — and I did several times. And quite a few times I have helped recover an aircraft on amphibs upside down in the water. During the 20 years I operated in Ely, Minnesota I would have four Cessna 172's on the line of 12 to 16 aircraft. The C172's I always ordered with overall aluminum with only a paint color stripe which saved just over 40 pounds. We used these for sightseeing with a couple going to surrounding lakes and resorts, some for training seaplane students, fire patrols and occasionally even hauling a party of two persons, canoe and their gear on short hauls.

I did check "Barnstormers" and found several Cessna 172's on floats for sale starting at $85,000.00. For a 150/160 h.p. ranging up to $160,000.00 for a 172 XP on Pk 2800 floats. I did see a 1966 model that was converted to a 220 h.p. Franklin engine with a constant speed propeller. This burns more fuel with a smaller useful load, but performs pretty well and had a decent paint job for $66,000.00. A Cessna 180 or 185 work well for a group of four adult persons, but I like the Cessna 206 that offers the sixth seat and more comfort room. The Cessna 206 could be installed on both straight (my recommendation) or amphibians. Edo, Pee-Kay, Wipaire or Aerocet usually have a couple of float sizes available.

If you are operating in an area with a large number of potential passengers, the DeHavilland DHC-2 Beaver is a good aircraft that will easily carry a pilot and six passengers and give them a stable ride. This is especially nice in higher winds and rough water. You will want one with the extended baggage that will give you more cabin space and window area. These are usually mounted on Edo 4930 or Wipline 6000 floats and will be sold for $250,000.00 to $300,000.00 if you shop around. I have owned 16 Beavers over the years and have almost 12,000 hours in the front seat — mostly the LH side, but have also given quite a hours checking out other pilots. We used to have people come to our business (Island Seaplane Service) in Hawaii to get checked out in the Beaver so they could negotiate a better rate from their insurance company when they bought one. My preference was the two bladed propeller even though the three blade was quieter.

The DeHavilland DHC-3 single engine Otter is another possibility if you want to move a lot of passengers. This would carry a pilot and ten passengers and still leap out of the water. When I was operating out of Ely, Minnesota for six or seven years in the winter I would take an Otter to Fort Myers, Florida and fly ten passengers every day to the Dry Tortugas Island (Fort Jefferson). This was a three hour flight round trip and we charged $150.00 per person. That was 50 years ago and the price would be much higher in todays market. On the return flight we would land in the harbor at Key West and give the guests a hour or so for lunch and a look see, then back up the coast with an overflight of the Everglades. This would be a 9:00 a.m. departure and a 5:00 p.m. return. I would pick everyone up in the morning on the causeway on Sanibel Island by heeling the aircraft back on a beach, but I started getting hassled by the City Attorney, so I kept the Otter off shore by a couple of feet and had the passengers wade out to the Otter — which settled that problem. There were 450 Otters built, so they are not something you see everywhere. Now most of them have been converted to turbine engines and the purchase price jumped to well over a million dollars. But if you shop around the Canadian side you can occasionally find one powered by the geared PW R 1340 piston radial engine for $500,000.00 to $600,000.00. These are usually pretty high time aircraft so you probably should plan on disassembling and completely go through the aircraft. I have owned seven of these and really enjoyed flying them and they were always a profit making machine.

After that a Cessna Caravan is the only choice and that does get into big bucks. They will run from 1.5 million to 2.5 million dollars on floats and usually have eleven to fourteen seats. Most of the ones you see advertised on floats will be on amphibious floats which will raise the purchase price and insurance and lower the performance and useful load.

ISLAND SEAPLANE SERVICE INC.
Honolulu, Hawaii
808-836-6273
seaplaneservice@aol.com   www.islandseaplane.com

Aloha,
   Our prices for 2018 will stay the same as 2017 NO increase. Here is the information on the price. Don't forget we are offering events working with groups. These have been very popular. We are offering a $179.00 per person pupu party with flight, minimum of 12 pax for this event. Also a $229.00 per person dinner party with flight minimum of 20 pax for this event. Please check out our website for more information.
Tax is 4.712

Price   ½ hour tour (Aloha Flight)
$179.00 + tax $8.43
-53.70 your 30% commission
125.30
+5.90 tax
$131.20 net to us

Price 1 hour tour (Islander Flight)
$299.00 + tax $14.08
-89.70 your 30% commission
209.30
+9.86 tax
$219.16 net to us

If you have any questions please call or e-mail us.

Warm Aloha's
Debbie Magie, Owner VP
Island Seaplane Service Inc.

Contact: Debbie Magie
Phone: 808-836-6273
Fax: 808-836-7861
e-mail: seaplaneservice@aol.com
We are closed 2 days each year. Thanksgiving and Christmas

CHAPTER 3

GETTING STARTED

If you have a spot with great natural beauty or a place of historical significance it is very simple — especially if there is a group of hotels to hold tourists. The simplest way to get customers is to approach the hotels concierge with a program of commissions, then they are happy to sell your flights. These could be as low as 10% of the price, but in Hawaii 30% was the standard commission for all activities.

But there were a zillion tourists and a hundred or so hotels on Oahu so we just raised our price to make a decent profit. We offered a one hour tour that flew around the island of Oahu. This would go down the length of Waikiki beach at about 1,000 feet in a slow climb to 1,500 feet which was the recommended tour flight altitude. In fact the FAA for awhile had Special FAR 71 that required tour operations to maintain a minimum of 1,500 feet AGL — only for Hawaii — so we would try to stay over water on our routes and give our passengers a closer look at everything. Then we would pass alongside of Diamond Head which was an extinct volcanic crater that had a tunnel through the wall that allowed people to drive inside to hike up to the rim and even had a sea cave on the ocean side. Then we proceeded east to Makapu'u Point where we turned north along the eastern shore past Kaneohe Bay Marine Corps air base, over Chinaman's Hat, Kaneohe Bay as far as Kahuku. We were operating under FAA Part 91 which allowed us to stay within 25 miles from our point of departure and no landings en-route, so we would turn left and proceed to Waimea and Haleiwa. Our last leg was southbound down the center of the island — past Schofield Barracks, Wheeler Army Airfield and Pearl Harbor as well as the route of the main Japanese attack force on December 7, 1941. It is very important to have a intercom with headsets for each passenger. We would brief the guests on a wall map before their departure to point out what they were going to see and then narrate the entire flight.

In Hawaii we sold a one hour tour for $299.00 per seat, which left us $209.30 after the commission was deducted. Of course if we sold the seats directly to the customer we got the full $299.00. We did have our own website which helped to direct customers to us. We sold a half hour tour for $179.00 per seat of which after commission we kept just over $125.00 per passenger. We did give complimentary transportation from the hotels we had contracts with using a 15 passenger van and a $10.00 per hour driver. This flight would take off in Keehi Lagoon, proceed down Waikiki Beach, Diamond Head Crater, to Makapu'u Point, then north to Kaneohe Bay followed by a 90 degree turn to the left going between the mountains through Pali Pass to Pearl Harbor. Then back to the sealanes for a soft landing at our base.

We also did a 20 minute tour to Diamond Head and back behind Waikiki to Pearl Harbor. We did not advertise this tour, but it was included in our meal deals or pupu parties. Once in a while we would take a direct booking for $99.00 per seat with a party of 12 persons. This would usually be two trips in the Beaver or almost $1,200 for 40 minutes of flying — not too bad! Hawaii had many sights that makes it pretty simple to get people interested in a flight. It took me eight years to get a permit to operate the only seaplane operation in the state. My wife and I operated for 23 years and leased a 50 foot wide by 300 foot long piece of property that our dock and office were attached to. The State raised the rent from $28,000.00 per year to $91,000.00 with a 20 day notice, so we moved on. I was 88 years old then and had lost my medical. You will notice I did not mention

Hawaii in this publication of places to operate, but the Airport finally lost all sense and is starting to closedown operators and airports. A naval Air Museum was closed down and Dillingham Airport on the North Shore was shut down putting several glider and skydiving operations out of business on a couple days notice following a crash of a Cessna L-19 tow plane. Several flight schools could not keep up with the rate increases and folded up. General Aviation is not well looked upon in Hawaii making it not a good place to make an investment.

The second most common use of a working seaplane is seaplane training for a single engine seaplane rating (SES). Of course this means that you should be a Certified Flight Instructor (CFI) with a SES Rating (this rating will also lower your insurance rates). To do this you should have quite a bit more time than just the rating. I actually had a few thousand hours on floats flying tours and charters when I got my original CFI. I was always too busy to bother with the CFI bit, but I got pushed into it and found out that I enjoyed it. Soon after that I added a CFII, multi engine seaplane instructor (MEI-S) and a multi-engine instructor land (MEI-L).

Here again there is a great variety of aircraft that can be used for training, but my favorite still is the Cessna 172 on floats. This also allows you to use the same aircraft for sightseeing tours as well as training. A lot of seaplane schools utilize J-3 Cubs or a Super Cub, but I have a great desire to watch the hands of the students. I have got almost 9,000 hours of flight instruction given — mostly SES and MES, but some instrument and only a few Private Pilot sign offs. In Hawaii we used a Cessna 206 for our SES training, but also did quite a few in the Beaver. We had a lot of people coming from the mainland and Japan, so they did not mind paying a little more to fly a working class aircraft.

The Cessna 180 can easily be used for both activities also or an Cessna 172 XP which has a 213 h.p. engine and higher gross weight and great performance. With an engine of 200 h.p. and a constant speed propeller allows using the aircraft for a original Commercial Pilot check ride. When

I started I bought a seaplane, I hired a pilot to teach me how to fly and took both my Private and Commercial rides on floats.

Another thing to think about is the matter of check rides for your students. The FAA is probably your first thought, but I have quite a few problems with their scheduling. The price is right —free, but I have had check rides scheduled two weeks in advance and the examiner did not show up. That can probably be handled if the affected student is local and lives nearby. It really creates a problem is the applicant has an airline flight to your school and allowed for only a few days. Or you might have a Designated Pilot Examiner (DPE) nearby, but you usually have to pay $300.00 or more for the check ride. This just raises the applicant cost which does not help your business. The best thing to do is have the FAA set you up as a DPE so you can handle these rides in house. This is quite handy because you can now do these even on weekends and holidays. This really helps when your student has traveled a longways to get to you. While we were in Hawaii we got quite a few seaplane students from Japan — and sometimes New Zealand or Australia. Being your own DPE will require you to have another CFI working for you — either full time or part time. It is not well looked on to do the training, sign off the recommendation, then do the checkride. If you have someone else do the last two or three hours of training and the sign off for the recommendation, you are covered.

The next thing to consider is the amount of training hours to do a rating. Fifty plus years ago we used a ten hour course that included one hour of solo. Now days you will not want to pay the insurance cost for the solo. We do not do a one day course because we want the applicant to see a variety of water conditions — smooth glassy water, rough water and cross winds. Most people seem to handle the course fine in that block of time, but sometimes a brand-new and low time Private Pilot might have to purchase another hour or two to complete the course. It is important to develop a reputation of turning out good seaplane pilots. Now I usually train for seven hours, then the check ride.

A couple of days ago I picked up a copy of the Seaplane Pilots Association magazine "Water flying".

This was a special edition with a directory of the operators offering seaplane instruction in the U.S during the year 2020. This showed the availability in just over thirty states and just under 100 operators and quite an assortment of different models of aircraft. What really grabbed my attention was the fact that the directory only listed <u>four</u> offerings of a multi-engine seaplane rating (MES). Not much competition in that market! One of these was in Alabama, another in Alaska, one in Minnesota and one in Nevada. I have almost 4,000 hours dual given in MES training — mostly in the Twin Beach 18's, but a little in the Grumman G-44 Widgeon and a few in a Grumman G-21 Goose, I have also flown the Piper Aztec Nomad on 4930 floats, the Cessna T-50 Bobcat on Edo 5870 floats which could not maintain altitude on one engine (which slightly increases your gliding distance), the Grumman Widgeon had a tendency to porpoise which they tried to cure by shortening and lengthening the hull. Also the Grumman Mallard—very nice but too spendy and the Dornier D-28A which handled nice on Edo 6470 floats, but the placement of the engine restricted external loads — no canoes or boats. For years I wanted to fly the Barkley-Grow on Edo 9225 floats — I did get to sit in one, but never did get to fly it.

I also flew the Australian GAF Nomad on Whipline 9300 floats. This was a nice machine with two turbines, but cost $600,000 50 years ago. I did come up with over 12,000 hours of MES anyway. As long as you are going to be in the seaplane training any, why not make a push for the multi engine seaplane business. Not only is there hardly any competition, but it is a lot of fun. MES brings up a unique maneuver that only shows up in the MES flights. This is the single engine glassy water landing. This is a touchy operation — you are below VMC and adding power on the live engine while feeling for the water.

Over the years I learned that there are three things in life that must be done very carefully! Number one is teaching a new AMES student Single Engine glassy water landings. This is not done in multi-land training. Number two is cleaning a porcupine for dinner, Number three is making love to a woman wearing spurs.

Once you make up your mind that you want to get into the MES business, you must decide how much to invest in the aircraft. If you look around Ontario and Manitoba you can find quite a few Twin Beechs on floats for sale. It was not too long ago there were six for sale in Fort Francis, Ontario and I think it was take your pick for $25,000.00. They had not flown for awhile so you would probably be looking at a double engine change and some float work. The fuel burn is 50 gallons per hour and the Pratt and Whitney 985 will use some oil. I loved the Twin Beech, owned four of them over 40 years. I personally put 11,500 hours flight time in them and my other pilots probably put another 30,000 hours in them. I modified them so that I could put two 17 foot canoes and six passengers inside the cabin. With no passengers I could fly five canoes — 2 ½ inside and 2 ½ outside.

Today I would personally be looking at a higher investment and go with some newer equipment like Piper Aztec Nomad which is built in Gravenhurst, Ontario (www.aztecnomad.com). This sold on either straight or amphibious floats with a left hand pilot door installed. They also offer three foot wing extensions, seaplane propellers and a 500 pound weight increase. This will make a 2200 pound useful load on straight Edo 4930 floats with a cruise speed of 135 knots, climb rate of 950 feet per minute and a stall speed of 49 knots and have a range of almost seven hours — and burn about 25 gallons per hour of fuel. Six seats are normal, but I have heard they got a 7th seat approval. Not only is this a terrific MES trainer to fly —light on the controls and quiet. This does make it easier and more enjoyable and the student will find it easier to retain what he or she learned. You can probably build up a charter business also if you have a Part 135 Certificate — especially with the seventh seat — a pilot and six passengers.

The Aztec has been around for many years and has a good reputation as a sturdy and easy aircraft to handle. I think the approvals start with the "C" model series. He used to say that would cost about $100,000.00 to convert your airframe and take three months or so. Dave Gronfors is the name of the owner of the company. I have a few hours in the Nomad and thoroughly liked it. The left door is a big thing for a seaplane. It also has a pretty good sized baggage compartment in the nose.

A working seaplane base does draw quite a bit of attention. When we built the base in Hawaii we quickly built a couple of eight foot tables and benches so that potential customers would sit and watch the take—offs and landings and give them the fever to try it themselves. We did not promote them bringing lunches, but we did not stop it either. We did develop a pretty good sideline doing dinner parties on the dock some evenings. These were mostly booked by different companies that wanted to give their employees a treat and a twenty minute seaplane tour was included. We usually served shiskebab or salmon and deep fried beer battered halibut with potato salad, corn on the cob and a dessert. The fare was $229.00 per person including the 20 minute flight and the booking company provided any alcohol. We needed a minimum of 20 persons for this activity and also had a pupu party with 12 or more people for $179.00 per person. Cheese and crackers, sausage, pot stickers, rolls, Maui potato chips with dip and other tidbits were provided. It seems to me that our largest dinner party hit almost 50 persons — which makes a profitable evening. We had a large dock of 225 feet long and 30 feet wide with palm trees and plants scattered on it. It made a very comfortable spot for doing such a event that they would do it a couple times per year as most of the guests really enjoyed this instead of sitting in a restaurant.

FLOATING OFFICE WAITING ROOM

STOCKING DISPLAY CASE WITH T SHIRTS BEFORE THE FINAL DECORATIONS

FLOATING BUILDING IN PROGRESS

CONTACT US

Email
info@aztecnomad.com

Phone
(705) 687-6696

24

CHAPTER 4

LOCATING PROPERTY

When you make a decision as to where to start your seaplane operation there are many things to be considered in the choice. One of the first things is an abundance of potential customers. This usually is by being located near a large city, but if the area has an unusual and famous attraction that draws many people that will work. 50 years ago I was operating in Florida during the winter months. I was based in the river in Fort Myers and one of my main activities was flying ten passengers (and me) in a DeHavilland DHC-3 single Otter from Sanibel Island to Fort Jefferson on the Dry Tortugas Island. This was a site of a prison in the 1800's. It was not quite an hour and a half going to the Fort where we spent about two and a half hours there and could see a lot of sea life in the moat. Then it was a 45 minute ride to the harbor at Key West for almost a two hour lunch and sightseeing. Followed by close to an hour back over the Everglades and landing at Sanibel Island at 5:00 p.m. I charged $150.00 per seat (ten seats) and they bought their own lunch at Key West. This was pretty good in those days, but would probably have to double it today.

When selecting a site you definitely want to be sure your chosen water area is legal for seaplanes. Throughout the U.S any major navigable river is OK according to the U.S. Coast Guard. This also takes in most saltwater areas. A lot of lakes are located near the cities, but most are manmade and they might not allow seaplanes. Some of them use these reservoirs for their drinking water and some of them are park areas. Seaplane Pilots Association ($59.00 annual membership) publishes a Landing Directory (888-772-8923) that pretty much lists legal waters.

If you are picking a large city just for the population size, try to get one that has at least one university or college and maybe a military base. This will offer a good source of young people that get out to do things. They will usually publish their own newspaper and you should subscribe and advertise your operation. Use your imagination and come up with some original ideas to bring flight customers, like Sunday morning breakfast flight for couples. You could specify a minimum of four couples with a breakfast of scrambled eggs with diced ham and onions, warm cinnamon rolls or bismarks with orange juice, coffee and tea. You could provide van service or they could do their own transport. Four people could fly at 0900 while four people eat, then switch at 0930 with the first four. Thus you have eight passengers for a 30 minute flight. This would also allow another four couples at 10:00 a.m. and be done by 11:00. You also want to get photos of this and get them published in the before mentioned newspapers.

Earlier I had suggested that on your property search you might find an operating airport that has one side fronting on the water. This may give you a chance to get a reasonable priced lease if you build a floating office and dock. You will have to come to terms with traffic patterns — you stay over water. My wife and I operated for 23 years on a lease from Honolulu International Airport which was even in Class Bravo airspace. We leased a 50 foot by 300 foot piece of shoreline, erected a fence and added water, power and a holding tank. Then we built a 20 foot by 40 foot office/home that was floating. We ended with a 30 foot wide by 225 foot long dock and complete with pneumatic ramps of 20 foot by 20 foot to get the aircraft out of the water for wash down when not being used. If you are located next to a fair sized airport you might look at a soup and sandwich spot for the employees for their lunch break with a 30 minute tour. Same thing, feed half while the other half flies. Evening dinners can be birthdays, engagement parties and holiday gatherings. Just keep your imagination going.

While we operated in Hawaii we accumulated several pets that we found our passengers enjoyed seeing. First one was a Muscovy duck (we named him Aflack) with a damaged wing that we found in our bushes one morning. We collected it and brought it down on the dock for food and water. Later that afternoon three more ducks swam in and waddled up our ramp. They were evidently a family group and settled in. Every morning and evening they would get a can of whole kernel corn served on the dock.

Then we found that would bring starving kittens in to feed on the corn at night. The first one was a small orange tabby who took a couple days of feeding her before she got trapped in our office — and ended up sleeping on our bed the first night. She is named Big Kitty and still lives with us. Then Marley—a very active calico cat was next when she showed up and went wild over a bowl of chicken and rice.

Then cat number three, Chuck—a-muck (a black and white Kitten) who was named after one of our favorite lakes in Alaska. The last one (a calico) had to be bottle fed by Debbie with an eyedropper to start with. She got named "Evinrude" because she had such a loud purr that when she would jump on the bed she would keep us up at night. The ducks brought a lot of attention. They were pretty messy, so we did not let them in the office, but they often lay in the doorway and the cats would simply jump over them to come in the house. The ducks loved the parties we had on the dock — especially the Bourbon soaked ice cubes! By the way, the cats kept down the number of mice and rats that usually show around floating installations and boats.

We had a lot of harassment from the airports divisions about the ducks. These were all white Muscovy which signified they were female — and could not fly. The male Muscovy had some very pretty green and black colors and could fly just fine. One day we had a couple of U.S. Fish and

Wildlife people come down on our dock fully armed and they were out on the dock taking pictures of the ducks.

I walked out and asked them what was going on, to which they answered that we could not have ducks there because they might fly into an airliner and cause a major accident. I did ask them if they knew anything about ducks and they answered "No". I told them that they were 100% white Muscovy which meant they were females and could not fly. The males were trimmed with a black and green scheme — very pretty — and they could really fly. The females would swim up and down the channel of Keehi Lagoon, but never lifted off the water. A woman friend brought us a male Muscovy (named Donald) one day but before long he flew away and we never saw him again. After a little over three years we got a certified letter from the airport manager, Jim Pratt, saying that if we did not get rid of the ducks they were going to revoke our lease. There was a woman on Duck Road in Kaneohe on the east side of Oahu who had 15 to 20 Muscovy ducks in her yard on one of the canals. We took 100 pounds of dry corn, some loaves of stale bread and our ducks to her. They had been a good asset to us and we missed them. The four cats stayed with us and came to America with us when we left Hawaii to check out snow in Montana — and are still with us in Washington waiting to go to Alaska. Most people do have their own pets, so they can help bring in customers.

As I said earlier that financially multi engine airplane training would be an excellent way to bring in quite a bit of money. I did MES training for almost 35 years and that was in the Twin Beech and that was expensive to operate with a 50 gallon per hour fuel burn, a 1,600 TBO on the engines and a high oil burn. Today I would look at the Piper Aztec Nomad. It has a high acquisition cost, but livable expense — only 25 gallons of fuel per hour and 2,000 TBO of engine time and a quart or so of oil per hour. It is a pretty neat aircraft to fly, responsive and has a left hand door for pilot access. Their literature says a 135 knots cruise speed with a seven hour range, a stall speed of 49 knots and can carry a useful load of 2,200 pounds on straight floats. I spoke with Dave Gronfors recently and he said they are test flying a Nomad that they just installed on floats and are hoping for a 180 top speed. I only had just under four hours in the Nomad, but I was really impressed. Another thought is that we required a prerequisite of a single engine seaplane rating before starting initial multi engine training to teach the basic water procedures. I found that about 50 % of our MES students needed to obtain the SES rating first — a little more income. I really enjoyed MES instruction. My last hour of dual was a sample check ride. Make the first take-off and lose an engine just before flight — abort! Another normal completed take-off, climb to 4,000 feet for stalls, steep turns, slow flight and single engine procedures. Then take-offs and landings — normal, cross wind, glassy water landing (usually simulated), single engine glassy water, step turns and the last landing would be a single engine. Then take off and fly back to our dock for docking and tie up. The FAA check ride the next day. I would think that you should charge $500.00 per hour or so for a seven hour course and then an hours check ride. This will bring in some good dollars.

MY FAVORITE DRIVER

BACK VIEW OFFICE AND CHAPEL BEFORE AWNING

CHAPTER 5

OPERATIONS FAR PART 91 AND 135

In my first operation in Ely, Minnesota I operated FAR Part 135 and Part 141 for just over 20 years. We did a lot of training for people with the GI Bill administrated by the VA and that required Part 141 flight training. I even ran a "Bush Pilot Course", throughout the winter months. We would start six students on September 15th and finish them up a few days before Memorial Day when I hired them to fly for the summer. They would fly floats for the first two months, finish up their Private Pilots License and some advanced water work. Then in late November switch to wheels during freeze up with the addition of skis during December. December, January, February and March would see the Commercial and instrument rating plus the Certificated Flight Instructor (CFI) in March and April. Then the Multi— engine land rating also in April and the multi-engine seaplane during May. We got a $10,000.00 deposit in September and then billed the VA monthly for 90% of their flight time. We guaranteed 400 hours of flight time in that 8 months and also provided a couple of house trailers on the property for their living quarters. They would go to work in May for the summer just before Memorial Day. Then they would be turned loose when the next group arrived in September, but maybe keep one of the best ones and the others would leave with 1,000 hours flight time and all of the ratings. Plus they get to help out in the shop with the aircraft maintenance and even man a snowplow keeping the entry road and a 3,000 foot runway usable on the ice all winter. They assisted in the changeover of floats, wheels and skis as well as pre-heating aircraft left outside when it was—40 degrees below zero or taking off in a loaded seaplane when it was 85 or 90 degrees above zero.

There are quite a few large flight schools around the country, but none of them could really know about a working aviation business such as this.

When we moved on to Alaska we only operated FAR Part 91. The GI Bill had expired and Alaska had a very sensible rule that allowed Part 91 operators that provided lodging and meals to transport their guests as long as it was done on one financial charge that included flying. We could even serve complementary wine with meals and did not charge for it. We did not do any flight training in Alaska for quite a few years, then started going to Northern California for the next ten years to do our major maintenance and a lot of single engine and multi—engine seaplane training. We would usually start this migration in late October and be operating before Thanksgiving. For several years we rented the same large house with a long dock — the owner went to Phoenix every winter. We would be there until late April and do all of our annual inspections on our six aircraft, any engine changes needed or paint jobs. It usually would be a three day trip without rushing and I must have personally made 50 trips between Cordova, Alaska and Lakeport, CA on Clear Lake. I hardly ever used a chart except in bad weather. We would usually buy 50 cases of wine at the spring sales in the California wine country. We would split these between the Twin Beech and the Otter so that we could fly non-stop from Seattle to Ketchikan and not have to deal with Canadian Customs and that volume of dutiable alcohol.

CHAPTER 6

MY START IN AVIATION

Pat Magie is known throughout the seaplane industry and has been involved in Seaplane training, for many years—both single engine SEA and multi—engine SEA. During all of those years he has said that almost all of the people say that it was the most fun of flying as well as one of the hardest to break into.

Looking for a job for someone else in the business means some tough prerequisites to qualify for insurance coverage. The other alternative is to start your own business which requires a large dollar and time investment, but allows many tax deductions. This also can be very rewarding — both financially and mentally.

Pat enlisted in the USMC in 1950 and spent almost two years there during the Korean War. He returned to Minnesota in 1952 to finish his college education and had an interesting business during the summer months guiding canoe parties around Northern Minnesota and Canada. This allowed him to realize his life's ambition at that time and make a two and one-half month one way canoe trip to Hudson Bay in 1955. He was guiding a young fellow from Texas who wanted to get toughened up for college football that fall. They were planning on using fresh fish daily for food until a waterfall incident that lost all of the fishing tackle — this changed the diet for the last month to porcupine. One porcupine would last for two days and then be replaced with another. It was a hard trip with a lot of portaging with no trails and shooting lots of rapids. They only saw other people three times in the entire trip — once at theOgoki River Hudson Bay post and then at the Albany River Hudson Bay post where it flows into the salt water and one native family in a canoe about four miles away across the lake they were on.

After he thought about it all winter, he decided that he wanted to see more of the north country and learn to fly to make it more possible. In 1956 he made a trip to Duluth, Minnesota and found two airplanes for sale. One was a 300 h.p. Gullwing Stinson and the other was a 75 h.p. Piper J-4 Cub Coupe side by side seating. The owner of the Stinson told him to buy a smaller airplane — a Cub or Champ, learn how to fly and then come back to talk to him. So Pat went back to the seaplane base and paid $850.00 for the plane, $1,200.00 for the pair of Edo 1320 floats, $179.00 for a new metal prop and $380.00 to install the floats and do an annual inspection.

He then paid someone to fly it to Ely where he hired Chick Beel — a USFS pilot to teach him how to fly. A year later he had soled on floats and skis — then sold the aircraft for $2,850.00 and made a small profit. He then quickly bought a four seat Stinson 108-3 for $5,500.00 including floats, wheels and skis.

Now he really learned about bush flying. The creed of the bush pilot was that if it did not fit inside — tie it on outside. Canoes, boats, lumber, plywood sheets. A few years later, he found out how to fly two airplanes at one time. It usually used a DeHavilland Beaver or Otter and dismantled the damaged aircraft. The engine, propeller, cowlings and control surfaces would go into the cabin, the two wings would be strapped back to back before strapping them down on the RH float and the fuselage on top of the LH float. It actually flew ok, but did not climb very rapidly.

The Stinson was kept two years and then sold for $6,000.00 and a 1955 Cessna 180 was purchased for $12,500 (N4636B) with Edo 2870 floats. This was shortly later listed on a FAA Part 135 certificate and a couple of contracts from the U.S. Forest Service for flying fire patrols and help on forest fires. The Cessna 180 was followed by a Howard DGA-15 on Edo 6470 floats (a poor man's Beaver). The Howard had a short wingspan and small flaps and was sold a year later and went to Greenville, Maine. This was replaced by a Twin Beech C-18s on 7850 floats in May of 1964. This seemed to be the first Twin Beech on floats registered in the U.S. (N6799C) By installing a cargo door and quite a few modifications inside the cabin made it possible to put two 17 foot canoes right inside and the installation of one folding canvas seat for five persons on each side it was possible to carry two canoes and six passengers inside. Now the business really took off.

He also bought a Piper Pa-12 with a 135 h.p. Lycoming engine, Edo 2000 floats and a set of Federal 2500 skis for $6,000.00. This was primarily bought as a training aircraft, but saw much service as a light charter aircraft also. In the spring of the second year he burned out an engine hauling a 16 foot wooden boat. The engine was overhauled and back in the aircraft during July. During the winter months and flying in—30 degree weather a lot of landing gear problems that required laying out on the ice welding the landing gear up to fly the next day. Finally the 2500 ski series were replaces with Federal 2000 skis. These were lighter and reduced a lot of the landing gear problems. Mid summer two cylinders went bad on the engine again. They were replaced and a deal made with a Cessna dealer to trade the PA-11 in on a brand new Cessna 172 (N4252L) sitting on floats in the show room of the Cessna distributor in St. Paul Minnesota. This was priced at $18,000.00 less $6,000.00 for the trade—in. This was a good move that immediately brought in almost a dozen new Private Pilot students. But best of all it opened the door to a Cessna Seaplane only dealership—one of three in the U.S. One was Bob Monroe of Kenmore Air in Seattle, another was Dick Folsom of Folsom Air in Greenville, Maine and Pat Magie of Wilderness Wings Airways in Ely, Minnesota. Pat started buying six brand new units in the spring for his own fleet with the dealer's discount, used them all summer and fall with hardly any maintenance that was not covered by Cessna, then sell them off during the winter for about what he paid for them — then another new order in the spring. This grew to ten units — usually four Cessna 172's, two 180's, one 185, two 206's and one Cardinal (usually a retractable 177). He was approached during the fall of 1966 and got his first new Cessna, a C150 on floats and one of the very first delivered. This did not work out to well with the 100 h.p. engine and a fellow in Minneapolis (Lee Gillagin of Crystal Shamrock Air Service) got an STC to install a Lycoming 150 h.p. engine. Pat talked to him, but there was a waiting list of a couple of months. As Pat thought about that he decided that after installing the conversion engine in the C150 he could purchase a new C172 that become standard with the 150 h.p. for a very few thousand dollars more and have four seats. As the years went on he would also have two Twin Beech 18's, a Noordyn Norseman, One DeHavilland single engine Otter and two DeHavilland Beavers on line. Over the years he has owned 16 Beavers.

CHAPTER 7

101 SPOTS TO CONSIDER

ALABAMA: GUNTERSVILLE (Lake) many resorts

GULF SHORE (Salt) large resort area—almost 200

FLORENCE (Tennessee River/Wilson Lake) college, convention center

TUSCALOSA (Black Warrior River) 2 colleges, airport on river

MOBILE (Salt—Downtown Airport—Broad Street) airport on river, college, convention center

ALASKA: KETCHIKAN (Salt) floating halibut house, cruise ships

JUNEAU (Salt) floating halibut house, cruise ships

SITKA (Salt) floating halibut house, cruise ships

VALDEZ (Salt) floating cabins, sightseeing

ARIZONA: LAKE HAVASU CITY (Colorado River/Lake Havasu) London bridge, resorts

PHOENIX (Roosevelt Lake) 3 colleges, strong military

BULLHEAD CITY (Laughlin Lake, Colorado River) many casinos

ARKANSAS: HOT SPRINGS (Hamilton Lake/Ouachita) airport on river, many resorts

BULL SHOALS (Bull Shoals Lake) many resorts

LITTLE ROCK (Arkansas River) Clinton Airport on river, Murre Lake, university

CALIFORNIA: LONG BEACH HARBOR (Salt) convention center, university, Queen Mary, 2 aquariums

LAKEPORT (Clear Lake) many hotels and resorts

SAN DIEGO (Salt-Seaport Village) convention center, 3 universities, strong military,

Navy, USMC, cruise ships

MORRO BAY (Salt) university, hotels, resorts

LAKE TAHOE (Lake Tahoe) many Hotels, resorts, ski areas

CONNECTICUT: HARTFORD (Connecticut River) airport on river, 3 universities

NEW LONDON (Thames River) airport on river, 2 colleges, US Coast Guard Academy,

ESSEX (Connecticut River) 2 museums

FLORIDA: FT. MYERS (Inter Coastal Waterways) Sanibel Island, all day tour to Tortugas Island & Key West

TAMPA (Salt) Courtney Campbell causeway, taxi to Tampa International Airport, work from restaurants

ST. PETERSBURG (Salt) Clearwater Airport, Part 135 Air Taxi

PANAMA CITY (Salt) airport has ramp to water, great beaches, Air Force Base

PENSACOLA (Salt) Pensacola Airport on water, national seashores, Navy Base, museum and many Hotels

GEORGIA: ATLANTA (Chattahoochee River) Fulton County Airport on river, many colleges, strong military

LA GRANGE (LaGrange Reservoir) college, Ft Benning 1 hour south

BRUNSWICK (Salt) Jekyll Island Airport on water convention center, water park, college

SAVANNAH (Savannah River/Hutchinson Island) 2 universities, Army

IDAHO: SANDPOINT (Lake Pendoreille/ Priest Lake) many resorts, seaplane history

POCATELLO (Pocatello Reservoir) airport on water, American falls University

ILLINOIS: QUAD CITY (Mississippi/Rock River) 4 colleges, convention center, history of seaplane service

PEORIA (PEORIA Lake) university, casino

CHICAGO (Lake Michigan) Navy Pier, good docking, history of seaplane use

BURHAM PARK HARBOR (Lake Michigan) McCormick Place, convention center

ROCKFORD (Rock River) airport on river, 2 universities

INDIANA: EVANSVILLE (Ohio River) used to be a seaplane base next to casino

KANSAS: WICHITA (Arkansas River) airport on river, 2 colleges, military

KENTUCKY: Kentucky Dam Lake/Barkley Lake, many resorts

LOUISVILLE (Ohio River) 2 universities, VA medical center

LOUISIANA: NEW ORLEANS (Lake Pontchartrain) airport on water, 5 universities, convention center

BELLE CHASSE (Mississippi River) many islands, floating cabins

MAINE: PORTLAND (salt) off East Portland Airport, Part 135, 2 universities

TRENTON (Salt) airport, Arcadia North Park, circle Island, Part 135—91

MARYLAND: BALTIMORE (Salt) Inner Harbor, Fells Pt, 6 museums and pavilions, World Trade Center, 6 universities

BALTIMORE (Salt) Essex just east of the main city, beaches

HAMPTON (Loch Raven Reservoir) north side Baltimore, 1 college

FREDERICK (Monocacy River) airport on river, AOPA headquarters, college, museums

MASSACHUSETTS: BOSTON (Salt) Lagoon Airport, Northside, Part 135,

EAST FALMOUTH (Salt) Martha's Vineyard, Nantucket Island, Elizabeth Islands, Part 135

SPRINGFIELD (Connecticut River) river airport, 4 colleges, military

MICHIGAN: HOUGHTON (River) Isle Royal National Park, Part 135

CHEBOYGAN (Mullet Lake/Burt Lake) Mackinaw Island, Bois Blenc Island

MINNESOTA: DULUTH (Sky Harbor Seaplane Base) training, sightseeing, 2 colleges

RANIER (Rainy Lake) training, sightseeing, Voyageur National Park

GRAND MARAIS (Devil Track Lake) training, sightseeing, transport to Isle Royal

MISSISSIPPI: GULFPORT/BILOXI (Salt) Big Lake or Back Bay, many hotels, casinos, convention center, military

VICKSBURG (Mississippi River) several casinos, hotels, convention center

MISSOURI: KANSAS CITY (Missouri River) Wheeler Down Town Airport, several casinos, 4 Universities, 2 convention centers, many hotels

BRANSON (Lake Taneycomo) many many music theaters, convention center, one College

LAKE OZARK (Lake of the Ozark) many resorts

MONTANA: POLSON (Flathead Lake) airport on the river, many hotels and resorts

WEST YELLOWSTONE (Hebgen Lake) sightsee Yellowstone National Park

NEBRASKA: OMAHA (Carter Lake) Eppley Airport on the lake, 2 colleges, several casinos, VA

Medical Center

NEVADA: LAS VEGAS (Lake Mead) many many hotels, casinos, strong military

NEW JERSEY: ATLANTIC CITY (Salt) intercoastal waterway, several casinos, 1 college, many hotels

OHIO: CINCINNATI (Little Miami River) Lunken Airport on the river, 3 universities

OKLAHOMA: TULSA (Arkansas River) Jones Airport, 3 universities

OREGON: NORTH BEND (Salt) airport SW on river, maritime museum

DIAMOND LAKE (Diamond Lake) north side of Crater Lake State Park

PORTLAND (Columbia River) Portland airport, 4 universities

LAKE OSWEGO (Willamette River) 4 universities

ASTORIA (Salt) Lewis and Clark Expidition, first to reach the Pacific Ocean

PENNSYLVANIA: PHILADELPHIA (Delaware River) Philadelphia Seaplane Base, 6 colleges

ERIE (Presque Isle Bay) convention center, 1 college

ALLENTOWN (LeHigh River) LeHigh Valley Airport, 4 colleges

HARRISBURG (Susquehana River) Capital City Airport, 2 colleges

READING (Schurlkill River/Blue Marsh Lake) airport on the river, 2 colleges

SOUTH CAROLINA: MYRTLE BEACH (Intercoastal waterwaysl) Grand Strand Airport on the river, 2 colleges

MYRTLE BEACH (Intercoastal waterways) airport, many many hotels

COLUMBIA (Lake Murray) 3 colleges, Military

CHARLESTON (Lake Murray) airport, 2 colleges, Fort Sumpter

TENNESSEE: NASHVILLE (Cumberland River) John Tune Airport on river, 4 colleges, 2 Convention centers, Grand Ol Opry

MEMPHIS (Mississippi River) General Spain Airport on river, 3 colleges, convention Centers, VA Medical Center

KNOXVILLE (French Broad River/Fort Ludlow Lake) McGhee Tyson Airport and Knoxville Downtown Island Airport, 2 colleges

DALE HOLLOW (Dale Hollow Lake) many resorts

CHATTANOOGA (Chickamaugh Lake) 1 college, convention center, prior seaplane operation on the lake

TEXAS: CORPUS CHRISTI (Salt) airport on the water in Bay, Padre Island National seashore, floating cabins, fishing

FORTWORTH (Eagle Mountain Lake) very scenic, training, sightseeing

DALLAS (Ray Hubbard Lake) both training and sightseeing

UTAH: PROVO (Utah Lake/Provo Bay) Provo Airport on water, training, sightseeing

VERMONT: BURLINGTON (Lake Champlain) airport near river, 2 colleges, National Guard

VIRGINIA: ROANOKE (Smith Mountain Lake) 1 college, VA Medical
Ctr, sightseeing, training

HAMPTON NEWPORT NEWS (Mill Reservoir) 2 colleges, military

NORFOLK (Salt) airport, 1 college, military

WASHINGTON: HOQUIAM (Salt) airport

WISCONSIN: ASHLAND (Lake Superior) Apostle Island National
Lakeshore, sightseeing

EAUCLAIRE (Chippewa River) airport on river, 1 college, training

CHAPTER 8

ALASKA 7 DAY TOUR

We once operated a seven day tour that flew around a good sized chunk of Alaska for sixteen years in June, July and August. We started Sunday about noon and came back Saturday afternoon. We used a Twin Beech 18 and a DeHavilland DHC-3 single Otter, both on floats with two pilots, one gal cooking and six guests. We provided practically all of the equipment and food — tents, the best we could buy that were easily movable every day, three inch foam pads, sleeping bags, tarps, cooking gear and even a hot shower that went up almost every night along with a axe and a thirty inch bow saw. At that time we were operating several outpost cabins in Prince William Sound and the Wrangell Mountains and a tent camp 100 miles down the coast on the Tsiu River. We also had a small lodge on Prince William Sound that offered saltwater fishing for Salmon, Dolly Varden, Halibut and Cod. This camp would hold fourteen to sixteen guests and another camp of the same size for Rainbow Trout, Lake Trout and Artic Grayling back in the Wrangell Mountains 100 miles north of Cordova. We used to sell that as a split trip—three nights at each camp with a Wednesday flight to exchange guests. During the summer months — June, July and August — we would try to keep the Tebay Lodge open on Sunday night and stop there to spend the first night of the tour with fresh Rainbow Trout for dinner. In the morning we topped off the fuel tanks on both aircraft and started north to the Nelchina Plateau and Landmark

Gap Lake. Landmark Gap Lake ran about five miles long north and south with steep mountain sides and excellent Lake Trout fishing — which we had for dinner that night. In the morning we could see a bunch of Caribou on the south shore and a couple of white spots to the North. These were Dall Sheep and we spotted them when we flew past, followed by a Grizzly in the water fishing as we passed over the river on the north end. Then we angled to the North East for Black River Pass and Delta Junction, then followed the Alcan Highway to Fairbanks for a fuel stop. The landing was on a manmade ditch of 5,300 feet long by 150 feet wide right in the middle of the airport and was labeled waterway 1 or 19 and the fuel truck would meet you at transient parking on the South end of 19 — very efficient! Then we started NE again to North Twin Lake. This was good fishing for Lake Trout and Artic Grayling, but we ate charcoaled New York Strip Steaks, baked potatoes, corn on the cob and chocolate banana pie. Not bad for North of the Artic Circle! The next morning we would fly Westerly to a small lake just off of the Artic Ocean. This had a nice sand beach that was shallow enough to get warm enough to swim — with the long Artic days — basically 24 hours of daylight. We were just North of the Kobuk River and we would take everyone over to fish for Sheefish and Grayling. Sheefish are a firm white meat and extremely tasty It used to be that the world's record came out of this river at 54 pounds. The next morning we had Eggs Benedict complete with Asparagus before we loaded up and proceeded south. We made a stop on the Yukon River at the village of Galena for fuel. This was always a interesting event because when our gal cook climbed out the back door and down the ladder, there would be twenty or twenty—five sled dogs there chained to posts and making a loud racket. We would be looking upstream while holding position with the RH engine idling while she tied the bow and stern ropes. The Yukon River had a strong current so after fueling we would take—off down stream and turn South, down the Innoku River to the Tikchick Chain of lakes where we landed on Chikuminuk Lake. Here we could fish for Salmon, but we had BBQed chicken, potato salad and fresh baked apple pie in the reflector oven. The next morning a short flight to Aleknagek for fuel, then Easterly up the Kvichak River to the 90 some mile long Iliamana Lake and stay at Kakhonak Lake. The next morning would start with a flight across Cook Inlet, the Kenai Peninsula, through Portage Pass at Whittier proceeding to our camp at Alice Cove on Prince William Sound. My daughter Katie would have a couple of our guides and boats there and some Salmon for dinner. I would drop the guests off and return to town. They would spend Saturday fishing for take home Salmon and Halibut. This way we got the use of the Beech 18 and the Otter to move our other guests going to our different camps on Sunday morning and all day Saturday. This was 40 to 50 years ago and we charged $2,495 per person and kept the trips pretty well filled. Alaska did not have a fuel tax and we could buy 80/87 octane (red) gas for not to much more than $1.00 per gallon and 100/140 (green) for a little more. We could even find a sale on a two pound slab of bacon with the rind attached for $2.00. Today the price would haves to be doubled at least. But the world has changed a lot for better or worse. I really think this could still work today seeing as it is the only way you can get around most of Alaska. We used to limit our flight time to about three hours per day with a landing every hour or so to fish different lakes or rivers or just to observe wildlife. We did this for 16 years and never did have much competition. One gal tried to do it with a Grumman Widgeon and a Cessna 206 Amphib, but she stayed in hotels in different villages or at fishing lodges that had room. She carried no camping gear, which I did not like. If the weather turned bad and she couldn't stay in civilization while we had the means to stay comfortable in almost any weather.

CHAPTER 9

FLOATING CABINS

Building floating cabins is not cheap, but can be financially rewarding because they are rarely found anywhere. You do need to find some protected water to anchor the cabin out. A small bay works well — especially if it has an island or reef at the mouth. If the location has some good fishing or hunting that is a good bonus that will definitely help you keep the units filled and revenue coming in. I had a business going in Cordova, Alaska almost 40 years ago when I built my first cabin. I built four each 2" X4" frames that were four feet wide by 4 feet high and twenty feet long and I covered them with ½" plywood sheets. Then I bought two barrels of liquid styrofoam, mixed it up and poured it in the floats. The next step was to seal the top of the floats and apply a heavy layer of fiberglass topped off with water sealant.

We built these in Lakeport, California while we wintered there while covering the U.S. doing sport shows selling our different trips. We then trucked the floats to Cordova, Alaska where we reassembled them into the forty foot long floats by bolting them together at the two flat ends. The other two ends were built with a two foot slant to make easier to tow around Prince William Sound. The entire frame was covered with two inch by twelve inch by twenty foot long planks to reinforce it and cover the deck with ¾" plywood to make a 20' X40' raft with an eight foot deck on each end and a two foot wide deck on either side. We kept a couple of 50 gallon plastic barrels filled with water on each side deck and refilled them a couple of times during the week. We used it for a six day week so that we had time to clean up and service the cabin. It became very popular, so I started building one every winter until we had five units. Occasionally we would get a reservation for a large group and we would bolt two cabins together — otherwise they were separated in different bays. Each cabin would have two fishing boats — a twelve or fourteen foot Livingston for which we took on as a dealership — a twelve or fifteen h.p. outboard motor. We provided the heavy duty fishing gear for halibut and showed everyone a couple of incoming rivers to fish for salmon during the incoming tide and then troll for halibut during the outgoing tides.

Each cabin got two crab pots and two shrimp pots which they would bait with the fish remains when they cleaned fish. We eventually added a twenty two foot covered C-Dory boat that we used for camp checks every other day to make sure everything was working and we would pick up fish to bring back to a walk-in freezer in town so they could take limits of fish home. The trip out and back from the cabins would be in an aircraft flight of ten or fifteen minutes — occasionally twenty minutes.

We started the cabin business charging $1,995.00 per person the first couple of years for six days and nights which included their food supply with New York Strip Steaks for the first night. By the time this fleet had increased to five units with the rate of $2,295.00 per person. A couple of years later wife Debbie and I sold my oldest daughter Kate and her husband Tom the entire business so that we could proceed to Hawaii to start a new business. A few years later they called and told us that all five cabins had sunk the day before after fifteen feet of snow in one day. The snow had piled up on the decks until it was just too much weight. This was a large chunk of their business and they went to the local bank and quickly got funded to build five new cabins. Now they charge $2,500.00 per person. They now bring them back to the harbor and lift them on shore for the winter.

I changed my design which actually is a lot roomier with a full upstairs which gives the cabin three bedrooms and two and one half bathrooms. The cabin is a twenty foot by thirty two foot building with no decks. A eight foot by sixteen foot float will be attached to the kitchen side with a small roof, table and BBQ for outdoor dining. The stove side will see a twenty foot by twenty—four foot float will allow an aircraft to dock there. These will have smaller (and cheaper) floats and be bolted to cabins so that they can be removed if there is a winter snow problem. The frame for the deck would be 4" X 12" treated beams and the floation sections fastened with lag screws under the frame. These would handle six guests and I suggest a minimum of four. The larger deck would hold fuel supply and a woodshed.

The propane would also be stored there and maybe a small propane freezer. If you are in a rainy area I suggest using a C-Dory 22 foot Angler and a C—Dory 16 foot Angler and give your customer a covered boat to stay dry in. Other than that would be hard to beat a Livingston 12 or 14 footer. They are wide and very stable as well as unsinkable. Either of these boats are available new or used. A string of these cabins will definitely make a DeHavilland Beaver on line to service them.

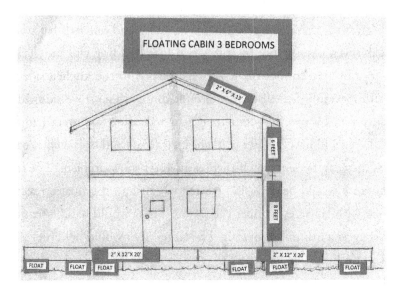

FLOATING CABIN 3 BEDROOMS

2" X 6" X 13'

6 FEET

8 FEET

2" X 12" X 20'

2" X 12" X 20'

FLOAT FLOAT FLOAT FLOAT FLOAT FLOAT

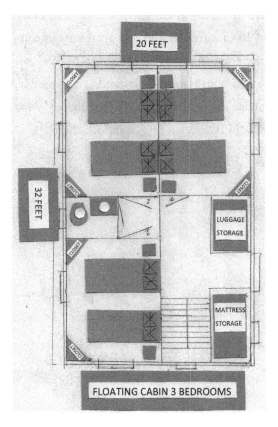

20 FEET

32 FEET

CLOSET

LUGGAGE STORAGE

MATTRESS STORAGE

FLOATING CABIN 3 BEDROOMS

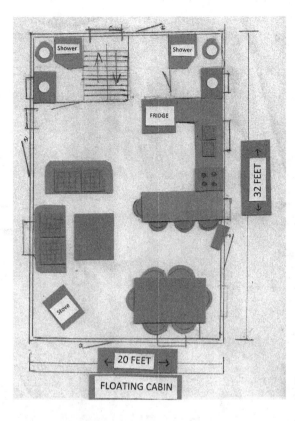

Shower

Shower

FRIDGE

← 32 FEET →

Stove

← 20 FEET →

FLOATING CABIN

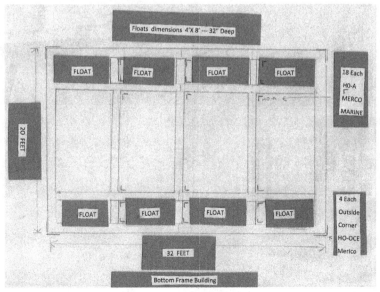

Floats dimensions 4'X 8' --- 32" Deep

FLOAT

FLOAT

FLOAT

FLOAT

18 Each

HO-A

MERCO

MARINE

HO-A

20 FEET

FLOAT

FLOAT

FLOAT

FLOAT

4 Each

Outside

Corner

HO-OCE

Merico

32 FEET

Bottom Frame Building

CHAPTER 10

BORN INTO AVIATION

My birth certificate reads April 29, 1930 and listed my father's name William Henry Magie II and his profession was Aviator. My mothers profession was Nurse. His father had graduated from medical school in Indiana in 1886 and hitchhiked to Duluth, Minnesota by horse and wagon and started a medical business which went very well. So my father was raised in a affluent family. He learned how to fly in 1920 at the age of 18 years. He then bought a Curtis Jenny — a two cockpit biplane. He was flying that out of a farmer's field for awhile until he was evicted for disturbing the livestock. He had heard that the City of Duluth was building an airport north of town and over the hill. He flew over there and sure enough there was a team of horses plowing a runway, so he buzzed the team to warn them he was going to land — and he did. 50 years later they were having a celebration of their airport and he was put up on the stage and introduced as the first pilot to land there — even before it was fully constructed. He finally sold the Jenny and bought a couple of seaplanes after he got grounded for three weeks for flying under the aerial bridge at the entrance to the Duluth Harbor when the bridge was up to allow a ship to enter the harbor, and started an air mail service between Duluth and Fort William, Ontario and all the villages in between along the North Shore of Lake Superior. This went pretty well for a couple of years until one of his pilots had to put down en-route for bad weather and did not tie the aircraft well and it sank. Then he got a job flying the U.S. Mail out of Eu Claire Wisconsin. My first ride in a airplane was at the age of four months which I don't remember — wrapped bundled in a blanket in a wicker laundry basket on my mother's lap in an open cockpit airplane from Duluth to Eau Claire, Wisconsin. This was the start of the Depression of the 1930's and his father lost a lot of money to the stock market and died in 1932. Franklin D Roosevelt became President in 1932 and by 1933 had started the road to recovery with the WPA and the CCC camps. Also my mother had one daughter and another on the way so the family started back to Minnesota. The U.S. Mail service was having quite a few accidents and by 1935 my father had a job as a foreman at CCC Camp out of Ely. The family moved into a large log cabin on Big Lake in 1935 — me and my two sisters with a third coming. My father bought me a single shot .22 caliber rifle to shoot partridges and rabbits to help feed the growing family and I would help him go out in the canoe to net fish at night. We soon got used to Bill Leithold with his Curtis Robin landing in front of the house to pick him up to go to a forest fire, During the summer of 1937 he drove me to Hibbing, Minnesota seventy miles away in our Packard to see one of his old flying buddies who was there hopping rides in a Ford Trimotor. We spent the whole afternoon with my father in the RH seat swapping stories while I sat in the wicker seat behind him. So airplanes were a big thing in all of my first years.

Who would have known that I would spend over sixty years and 40,800 hours making a living flying seaplanes.

ABOUT THE AUTHOR

The year is 1952 and the U.S. Marine Corps has just turned Pat loose upon the civilian population. Magie heads to northern Minnesota, where he traps wolves for bounty and leads canoe trips into the wilderness. Highlight of this era is a 2 ½ month pilgrimage to Hudson Bay. A menu of porcupine and rice keeps the Hudson Bay explorers alive while they paddle and portage their canoe throughout the North.

During the Hudson Bay trip, Pat developed a keen interest in the far north. To explore further, he concluded that air travel was the way to go, so he bought a Piper J-4 Cub with floats. Flying lessons followed, with solo in eight hours and a solo cross country endorsement obtained aboard a Forest Service Beaver.

For first solo cross-country, Pat decided upon a lake up north with some duck-hunting thrown in for good measure. Timing could have been better however, for this lake froze overnight and takeoff from the remote location was not possible. Pat let the lake freeze hard over, chopped the plane out of the ice, coaxed it onto the ice and took off, floats skating across ice until liftoff speed. Upon returning home, Magie landed on ice with the floats, then switched to skis for winter's duration.

After 485 hours of adventures it was time for the commercial check ride. This required a flight from an airport and Pat's first landing on wheels took place that day.

A series of float planes followed the Cub-a Stinson, Cessna 180, and Howard DGA15. Pat then added the first Twin Beech ever to operate in the U.S. with floats. The beauty of the Twin Beech was that it could carry two canoes at a time and his Wilderness Wings business thrived, opening up vast portions of Northern Minnesota to adventurous canoe enthusiasts. Pat also sold float-equiped Cessnas, and he could get a plane headed north sometimes in the same day the order was received.

Alas, the federal government created a wilderness area which eliminated much of his business, so in 1980 Pat headed north to Alaska, flying for some of the same outfits which bought planes from him earlier.

In 1989, Pat Magie visited Hawaii for the first time and decided the place offered promise. It took years working through bureaucratic thickets, but he and his wife have now established their Island Seaplane business. The Beaver mostly takes sightseers aloft. The Cessna 206 performs this role as well as giving land pilots a chance to earn a seaplane rating. Pat doesn't believe in quicky courses and he'll leave you with an impression of glassy-water landings which may save your life someday. In 2018 the State raised rent 400% thus shutting the business down.

Pat does hold the world record of more hours flying seaplanes than anyone in the world. Over 33,000 hours in seaplanes with a total of 40,000 hours of accident free flying time. He is also a well respected seaplane stunt pilot for many movies and TV shows. His father Bill Magie had the first comercial seaplane operation in Minnesota and held flying license # 8 signed by Orville and Wilbur Wright. All of his 4 children have ended up in Aviation.

My first book: WHATTA LIFE is a compliation of stories (38 chapters) about my life and businesses in Aviation along with many adventures with many lives saved in middle of the night med-avacs by seaplane along with seaplane stunt flying for movies, TV shows and comercials.

My aviation businesses are as follows:

Wilderness Wings Airway in Ely MN in business for 20 years
Alaskan Wilderness Outfitting Company in Covdova Alaska for 20 years
Island Seaplane Service Inc. Honolulu, Hawaii 23 years
Seaplanespecialist LLC one year
I started all these businesses from the ground up.

Printed in the United States
by Baker & Taylor Publisher Services

225 feet of dock, 2 pneumatic ramps for aircraft parking, 2 20 by 30 foot hinged ramps to hold positioning of a 20 by 40 foot office/home and a 20 by 24 foot wedding chapel secured to a 50 foot by 300 foot piece of leased property.

THE AUTHOR SPENT 63 YEARS IN THE SEAPLANE BUSINESS WITH OPERATIONS IN NORTHERN MINNESOTA, FLORDIA, CALIFORNIA, WASHINGTON, ALASKA AND HAWAII. HE HAS OPERATED FAA PART 91, PART 135, PART 141 AND HAS EVEN HELD A CANADIAN 9-4 UNSCHEDULED CHARTER CERTIFICATE. HE FLEW 40,800 ACCIDENT FREE HOURS INCLUDING A RECORD 33,000 HOURS ON FLOATS. HE HAS CONSTRUCATED MANY SEAPLANE DOCKS AND TWO STORY FLOATING CABINS - SOME WITH UP TO FOUR BEDROOMS.

ISBN 978-1-6655-1751-5

authorHOUSE®

TRUE ESSENCE

DANITA STEWART